Have You Started Yet?

Ruth Thomson is an award-winning writer of non-fiction books for both children and young people. She writes on an eclectic range of topics, including history, writing skills and art and design, as well as on the human body and health. She also travels widely, collecting recycled artefacts and stories about their makers to exhibit in museums and galleries.

Chloë Thomson is a psychology graduate with a particular interest in eating disorders, teenagers and health. She has worked on the development of leaflets and posters for several health campaigns for a major cancer charity. Chloë currently splits her time between writing and working as a camera assistant for both television and film.

Have You Started Yet?

You and your period: getting the facts straight

Ruth Thomson with Chloë Thomson

Illustrated by Jane Eccles

MACMILLAN

First published 1980 by Pan Books Ltd

This third revised edition published 2010 and reissued 2013
by Macmillan Children's Books
a division of Macmillan Publishers Limited
20 New Wharf Road, London N1 9RR
Basingstoke and Oxford
Associated companies throughout the world
www.panmacmillan.com

ISBN 978-1-4472-2611-6

1 3 5 7 9 8 6 4 2

A CIP catalogue record for this book is available from
the British Library.

Typeset by Josephine Spencer
Printed and bound by CPI Group (UK) Ltd, Croydon CR0 4YY

Contents

For my mother, Cynthia Walton

Acknowledgements

The authors would like to thank the three hundred or so girls, boys and women whose detailed answers to questionnaires and interviews form the backbone of this book. They would also like to thank the following individuals and organizations for their help, advice, constructive criticism and encouragement: Cynthia Walton; Natika Halil (Director of Information services, FPA); Helen Cameron; Sally Martin; Dr Stephanie Lamb; Ask Brook team; Hazel Slavin; Lynda Measor; Woodcraft Folk; Bizzy Walton; Poppy Walton; Mike Shields BSc, FRCS, MRCOG; Pam Chrismas; The Kids Book Group (Catherine Brighton, Nicci Crowther, Anita Harper, Ann Heyno, Christine Roche); Bhupinder Sandhu MBBS, MRCP; Gill Haymer; Ruth Parrish; Judy Bastyra; Barry Scherer; Dr Ellen Goudsmit; Pippa Cleator; Gail Chester; Jane Jenks; Elinor Williams; Roy Pennington; Miss J. M. Baugh; Catherine McManus; Roger Lawrence; Nicola Ruck; Robinsons of Chesterfield; Mary Abbott of Kotex Products Advisory Service; Tampax; Grapevine; Janice Saunders; Debbie Miller; Joyce Rosser (Deputy Director of the FPA Education Unit); Dilys Went (Lecturer in Human Biology, University of Warwick); Diane Jameson of Smith and Nephew; Coralie Tiffin; Joan Walsh (Health Policy and Research Officer, FPA); Anna and Judith Shipman; Subashini Puvanendrampillai; Alex Hegazy; Ivana Mackinnon; John Coleman (Director of the Trust for the Study of Adolescence); Joanna Coleman; Alys Fowler and Mia Morris.

Introduction
What's This Book About?

This book is about the changes that girls experience some time between the ages of eight and seventeen. It is particularly about periods, something that every woman in the world has for thirty or more years of her life. It will tell you how and why periods happen, what they are like and what to do about them. It gives practical suggestions for dealing with possible problems, and answers all sorts of questions girls often ask.

Before we wrote this, we sent out hundreds of questionnaires, went to lots of schools and interviewed many women, girls and boys to discover what their experiences had been like and to find out what they wanted to know about most. We have included a lot of their quotes throughout the book, so that you can see how enormously experiences and attitudes differ.

This book has been written for girls, but it would be helpful for boys to read it too. Girls often feel that periods are a secret they must keep from boys, but the more boys know, the better they will understand girls' feelings and the less embarrassed and awkward they may feel themselves.

Don't feel you have to read the book all at once. It's been written for you to dip into as a reference book, to find out things as and when you need them. Share it with your friends and be bold enough to pass it on to a boy!

Chapter 1

Starting Your Periods

At some time, usually between the ages of eight and seventeen, girls start having periods. The scientific word for periods is menstruation (pronounced men-stroo-ay-shun), but people often a use slang word or phrase instead – such as being 'on', 'coming on', 'monthly' or 'that time of the month'.

What is a period?

A girl's first period is a sign that her body is getting ready to be able to have a baby. The thing that tells her that her periods have started is blood appearing from an opening between her legs, called the vagina (to find out what this is, turn to page 31).

Will starting my periods change me?

Usually blood is a sign that there's something wrong with your body, like a cut or a graze. But when you have a period there's nothing wrong with your body and you haven't hurt yourself. In fact, quite the reverse. Your first period shows you that your body is developing and working in a new way, exactly as it's programmed to do. Starting your periods doesn't change you overnight, nor does it mean you have to behave any differently from before. It's just one of the many changes that will happen to you as you grow up.

Will I have periods forever?

You will have periods as long as you're fertile (able to have a baby). Once you've started your periods, you're likely to have one every month – but periods usually stop when a woman is pregnant – until you're in your late forties or early fifties, when they will become less frequent and then stop entirely. This is called the menopause.

Talking about periods

The more you know about periods, the better prepared you'll be when they happen to you. Although this book should give you most of the information you need to know, it's a good idea, if you can, to share your ideas and feelings with someone you're close to, such as your mum, an older sister or cousin, your dad, gran or carer, just as these girls did.

A girl at school told me she bled regularly and had to wear something to deal with it. She said all girls had it eventually. I couldn't believe it. I thought she had some terrible disease and had been told this story to console her. I told my mum what she had said and asked if it was true. She said it was and told me all about periods.

My sister was really nice to me when I started my periods. We didn't used to get on generally – she was eight years older than me. She gave me a sanitary towel and showed me how to put it on. That was nice. It felt like I was being looked after.

Chapter 2

Why Is My Body Changing?

Up to about the age of eight or nine, girls and boys have similar-shaped bodies, with no real waist or hips, and slim shoulders. They both have flat chests with small nipples and their voices sound similar. They have the same organs for breathing, moving and digesting food. As they grow, all their organs grow too, but they don't change in any way.

Puberty

....

At some time after the age of eight, often at eleven or twelve, girls' and boys' bodies start changing. This time of change is called puberty. The changes mean their bodies are getting ready so that they'll be able to have children when they're older. It doesn't mean everyone will automatically or necessarily have children. That choice will be up to them, when they're ready to make it.

BEFORE PUBERTY

Why does puberty happen?

At puberty, a tiny gland at the base of the brain, called the pituitary, sends chemicals, called hormones, into the bloodstream. These reach the sex glands and start them working. In girls, these glands are called ovaries and in boys, testicles. These glands, in turn, start to produce hormones of their own, which trigger off sexual changes to the rest of the body. As a result, women and men end up looking different.

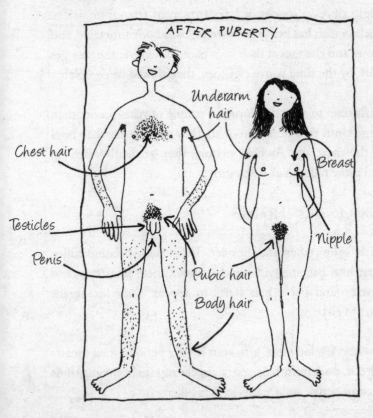

AFTER PUBERTY

Chest hair

Underarm hair

Breast

Testicles

Penis

Nipple

Pubic hair

Body hair

HORMONES

Hormones are like chemical messengers. They are produced in one part of the body, usually the glands, then they travel around the body giving messages to cells and organs.

How quickly will my body change?

The changes don't happen to everyone at the same time. You might develop sooner or later than your friends or sisters. Each person has her or his own in-built body timetable, and grows and changes at their own pace. Whenever the changes start, by the time you're eighteen, they should be complete.

Girls tend to start developing a couple of years sooner than boys. Until they're fifteen or so, they grow faster than boys of the same age. As boys mature, they gradually catch up and grow taller than many girls.

How do girls change?

Girls grow taller and heavier. Their faces become fuller, their hips become wider and rounder, their breasts start to develop and pubic hair starts to appear. Their sex organs start to change.

As they develop more, girls start having periods, their breasts fill out, underarm hair starts appearing, their sweat glands become active and their skin gets oilier.

Your changing body

Before puberty you grow so slowly, year by year, that you've probably scarcely even been aware of growing. At puberty, you'll notice a sudden surge and, in a way, you have to get to know your body all over again. As you become aware of your own body, you'll probably also become more aware of other people's. You may worry that some bit of you isn't quite how you'd like it to be, but just remember that almost everyone else is worrying too!

EATING DISORDERS

Some girls worry so much about their weight that they become obsessed by dieting and exercise. Anorexia nervosa and bulimia nervosa are eating disorders that are the extreme of this. Those suffering from anorexia develop a fear of becoming fat and see themselves as fat even though they are actually very thin. They may starve themselves or over-exercise in an attempt to control their weight. Those suffering from bulimia also have a fear of becoming fat. They binge on food then make themselves sick to maintain a certain weight.

Anorexia and bulimia can have severe long-term effects on the body. Being a very low weight for a prolonged period of time can make periods very irregular or stop entirely, and can affect fertility in the future.

If you're feeling worried about your weight, it's important to share your concerns. Try speaking to your mum, dad or carer, or discussing your worries with your doctor. There are various support networks and helplines (see page 111) that specialize in supporting young people with eating disorders.

Growing taller and heavier

In the year before your periods start, you're likely to put on about 11 lb (5 kg). In the following years, you may put on another 8–12 lb (3.5–5.5 kg) a year until you reach your adult weight. This weight gain is absolutely normal. It does not mean you're going to end up fat, because you'll be growing taller and your limbs will be growing longer at the same time.

If you want to keep yourself in good shape, these tips might help:

❀ Eat plenty of fresh fruit and vegetables.

❀ Limit sugary and high-fat foods like chocolate, cake and biscuits.

❀ Exercise regularly.

Growing breasts

Growing breasts is one of the first changes you're likely to notice. This is a completely natural part of puberty and a sign that your body is doing just what it should. To begin with, you will develop breast buds – small hard lumps behind each nipple. Then the coloured area around your nipples will become larger, darker and stand out. These may become very sensitive to touch. Then, gradually, your actual breasts will develop. Some girls notice a tingling feeling or occasional soreness as their breasts grow – this is entirely normal. Some girls are pleased when their breasts start growing, others feel self-conscious.

When will my breasts grow?

Girls grow breasts at different ages – some at nine, and some at seventeen, and most girls somewhere in between. Any age is normal.

I HAD BREASTS AT TEN AND WAS AMAZED HOW
JEALOUS SOME GIRLS WERE IF THEY DIDN'T HAVE
BREASTS AS LARGE AS THE NEXT GIRL. WE ALL
COMPARED SHAPES AND SIZES.

I felt really
proud. I often measured
how much they'd grown
and couldn't wait
to wear a bra.

I didn't really like
my boobs growing.
I knew I'd have to
wear a bra and I
felt embarrassed.

How big will my breasts grow?

Breasts, like other parts of the body, come in all shapes and sizes. There's no such thing as 'perfect' breasts, even if magazines and adverts try to persuade you otherwise. If your mum and female relatives (on either your mum's or dad's side) have small or large breasts, the chances are that your breasts will end up a similar size to theirs.

If you have small breasts and have had periods for several years, your breasts are unlikely to grow much bigger. If you've only just started your periods, or not started yet, and your breasts are growing, you can expect them to grow some more. Some girls' breasts develop quite quickly, others take a few years to reach their full size. You can't do anything to speed the process up or slow it down, but wearing a comfortable bra in the correct size and having good posture will make the most of what you have, whether your breasts are large or small.

Is it normal to have one breast bigger than the other?

Breasts don't always grow evenly. Sometimes one grows faster than the other. Don't worry – they will more or less even out in time. It's perfectly normal if one of your breasts is slightly larger than the other – very few women have two breasts exactly the same size. Even if your breasts don't exactly match up, it's very unlikely that anybody else will be able to tell the difference.

Pubic and body hair

When your pubic hair first starts growing, it is soft and colourless. Eventually it darkens and coarsens. It is usually darker than the hair on your head, or may be a different colour altogether. Some girls have quite thick pubic hair, others have hardly any.

Hair will also start growing under your arms and on your arms and legs as well. It is not unusual to find hair growing around your nipples or across your tummy.

Your sex organs

As well as your changing size and shape, some parts of you develop in new ways. For instance, your vulva (external sex organs) becomes larger and more sensitive.

Getting to know your body

If you've never had a close look at your vulva before, it's worth spending a quiet moment getting to know what it's like and then seeing how it changes. The more you get to know and value your body, the better you'll feel about it. You'll also find it useful if you want to try using tampons during your periods (see page 61).

Make sure you're not in a rush and have a bit of privacy and clean hands. You'll need a mirror and a good light. Sit on the floor, or a bed, with your legs apart and your knees bent. Hold the mirror up between your legs and prop this book where you can see it easily. See if you can identify everything from the picture on the next page.

Remember, though, girls' vulvas differ as much as every other part of their bodies, so your vulva might not look exactly like this one. Your lips might be bigger or smaller or you may not have a hymen.

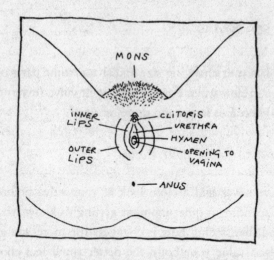

The mons is a fatty pad which protects the pubic bone inside. It becomes covered with pubic hair.

The outer lips are folds of fatty tissue, which protect the inner area and keep it moist and healthy. They become covered with pubic hair on the outside. During puberty, they gradually become larger, darker, fleshier and sensitive to touch.

The inner lips are the folds of tissue you will see if you gently part the outer lips. They are hairless, moist and may be pink or brown. Usually they lie together and protect the opening during puberty. You may have inner lips which stick out beyond the outer ones, one lip longer than the other or very small ones. All of these are quite normal. At the top of the lips, the folds are joined together and cover the clitoris.

The clitoris is the most sensitive part of your vulva. You'll only be able to see its tip, a bump about the size of a pea. The rest is hidden under the inner lips. If you can't find the clitoris, gently press around where you think it should be. When you notice a pleasant sensation, you've probably found it.

The urethra (urinary opening) is a tiny hole just below the clitoris, where your pee comes out.

The opening to the vagina is the bigger opening below the urethra. It looks quite small, but can stretch a great deal. It leads to the uterus (womb) inside your body. It is where the flow of blood comes out during a period.

The hymen is a thin stretchy fold of skin which may partly cover the opening to the vagina. Usually there are one or more openings in it through which blood can flow during a period. In the past, people thought they could tell a girl was a virgin if her hymen was unbroken. In fact, many girls are born without a hymen at all. A girl's hymen is often stretched or broken naturally by exercise, such as running or riding a bike. Virginity has nothing to do with whether you've got a hymen or not. You stop being a virgin only when you have sexual intercourse.

The anus is the opening through which poo comes out of your body. It is not part of your sex organs.

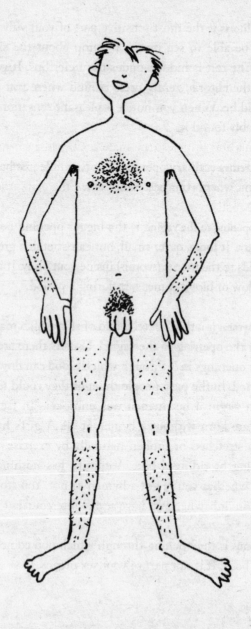

How do boys change?

Boys grow taller and stronger and their feet grow bigger. Their shoulders broaden, their chest widens and muscles start to develop.

The penis and testicles (the male sex organs) start to grow bigger and pubic hair starts to appear. The testicles start producing sperm (male seeds). Often, the skin around the testicles reddens and coarsens.

As boys continue to grow, their vocal chords grow. This eventually makes their voices deeper, although they may squeak from time to time at first.

Hair starts growing under their arms, on their faces and perhaps on their chest as well. The hair on their arms and legs grows thicker and darker and their pubic hair becomes thick and curly. New sweat glands develop and start working.

Chapter 3

Why Do Girls Have Periods?

As well as all the changes you can see happening, other important changes, that you can't see, are happening inside your body at the same time.

All about your reproductive organs

The reproductive organs that you were born with start to grow and develop. Each one is designed to play a part in producing a new life – whether or not they ever do so.

The reproductive organs are well protected inside your body.

To find out precisely where they are, put your forefingers on the bone just above where your legs meet. Now put your thumbs on the front of your hip bones.

Your reproductive organs are enclosed inside this bony area. They are a similar size for everyone, regardless of body size.

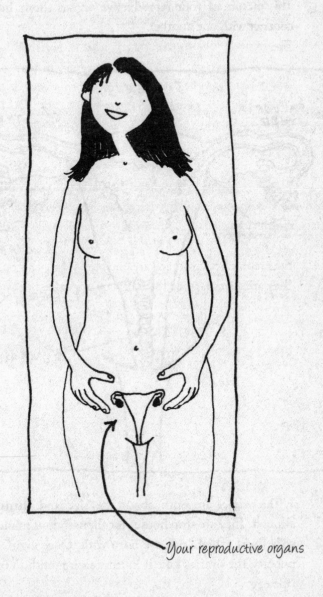

Your reproductive organs

This picture of your reproductive organs shows how they connect with one another.

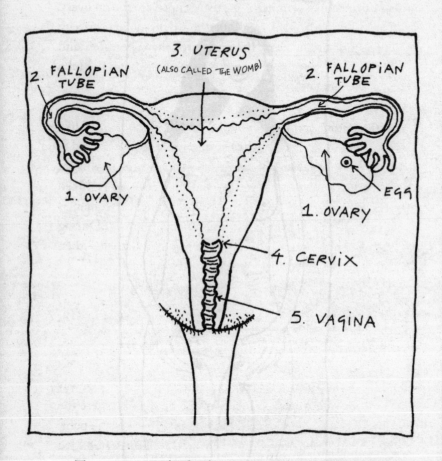

1. The ovaries are both about the size and shape of an almond. They are storehouses for thousands of minute egg-cells (ova), which girls are born with. Once a girl reaches puberty, the ovaries take it in turn each month to release a ripe egg.

2. The Fallopian tubes are each about the length and thickness of the inside of a ballpoint pen. One end, fringed and shaped like a funnel, is partly wrapped around an ovary. The other end opens out into the uterus. When an egg comes out of an ovary, the fringes of the tube catch and draw it into the tube. The egg then travels through the tube towards the uterus.

3. The uterus (womb) is a hollow, stretchy organ, shaped like an upside-down pear. It has strong walls of muscle and is lined with glands and blood vessels. It starts growing bigger when you're about ten and by the time you are eighteen it will be the size of a clenched fist. When a woman is pregnant, this is where the unborn baby grows. During pregnancy, the uterus grows to the size of a netball – then goes back to its normal size again after the birth.

4. The cervix is the entrance to the uterus. It usually stays closed. It opens slightly during a period to let the menstrual blood trickle out, and only fully when a baby is born.

5. The vagina (also called the birth canal) is the passageway from the uterus to the outside of the body. It is where the flow of blood comes out during a period. It is where a penis will enter during sexual intercourse. Its walls of soft, folded skin stretch very easily to allow a baby to be born.

The menstrual cycle

The menstrual cycle is the number of days between the start of one period and the next. It may be as short as twenty-one days, as long as thirty-five days, or anything in between. In this diagram we have used the average cycle length (twenty-eight days) to give an explanation of the menstrual cycle, but having a cycle shorter or longer than this is perfectly normal.

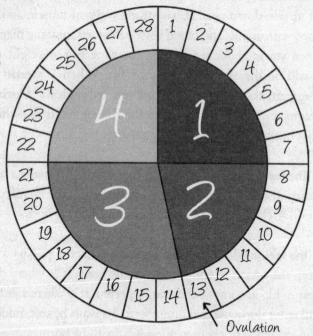

Ovulation

The life of an egg-cell

Once you start having periods, this is what happens inside your body every month.

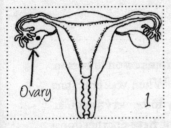

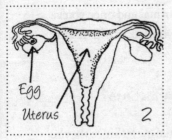

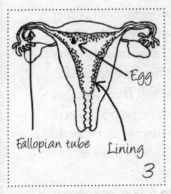

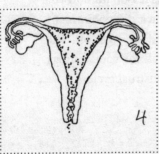

Ovary **1**

Egg
Uterus **2**

Fallopian tube *Lining*
3

4

1. At about the time your period stops, a tiny egg-cell starts to ripen in one of the ovaries. The following month, an egg-cell will ripen in the other ovary.

2. The ovary sends a hormone signal to the uterus. The lining of the uterus begins to thicken. About fourteen days after your last period, the ripe egg bursts out of the ovary. This is called ovulation.

3. The egg travels down a Fallopian tube towards the uterus. By now the lining of the uterus has become thick and spongy to make a soft bed for the egg if it becomes fertilized. But the only way an egg can become fertilized is if it joins with a sperm. This can happen if sperm comes into contact with the vagina in any way.

4. If the egg is not fertilized, your body knows that it doesn't need the spongy lining, which breaks down. The blood vessels contract, causing bleeding. The lining and the remains of the egg flow out of the uterus and through your vagina. This is your period.

How long is a menstrual cycle?

The length of a menstrual cycle varies from person to person, and may vary from month to month. When you first start your periods, your cycle is quite likely to be very irregular. You might have a period and then not have another for a couple of months. This is completely normal and once you've been having your periods for a while, your cycle will usually settle down.

How does my menstrual cycle affect me?

Periods are only one part of the menstrual cycle. Since they're the part that seems most noticeable, girls often don't bother to think about what's happening to them during the rest of their cycle. But perhaps you've noticed that on some days you feel great, have bags of energy, can do things especially well and that your skin and hair look good. Then, on other days, you feel awful – you can't concentrate properly, you're clumsier, feel pain more, snap at your parents and friends, feel low or sad about the way you look and cry more easily.

Sometimes, of course, there is an obvious reason for how you feel. Maybe you've had a celebration or a disappointment, or perhaps you've been complimented or told off. But sometimes you can't see any reason at all for your feelings. There is one! It's all to do with your menstrual cycle.

Sometimes my nipples hurt the day before I come on. I get constipated for the first few days and I get cramps.

I feel I can't do much when I have periods, and I get annoyed.

On the other hand, you might feel OK most of the time, except around the time of your period.

I don't notice any changes in mood due to my periods. I'm very moody anyway and my moods change from hour to hour and day to day without any reason that I can see.

You may be aware that your moods change noticeably at different times of the month.

I feel very high after a period, then, just when I think I'm going to do great things in the next few weeks, I get low. Now that I know what it is, I try to plan for it.

Or you might feel good for most of your cycle except for the week or so before your period is due. Then you might notice changes to your body, such as:

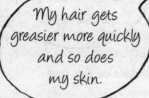

My hair gets greasier more quickly and so does my skin.

My boobs get bigger and my tummy feels tender. I feel heavy and fat and get spots.

Your moods may change at the same time.

I'm impatient and snap at people for no reason.

I feel stupid and slow.

I'm miserable a week before I'm coming on. I get a bit quiet.

I feel grumpy, uncomfortable and cry easily.

USE A DIARY TO KEEP A CHART
OF YOUR FEELINGS

Find out whether and how your cycle affects you by keeping a record of your feelings. After three or four months, you should be able to see whether any particular feelings happen again and again at the same intervals.

Keeping a chart of how you feel will help you work out the days when you might feel a bit down. Then you can prepare for them and not arrange too much to do. You may also find that once you know why you're feeling a certain way, you can cope better with those feelings anyway.

✿ Mark each day of your period with a P.

✿ Mark days when your flow is heavier with an H.

✿ Note the days when you feel particularly good or bad with your own symbols, pictures or words.

✿ Weigh yourself the week before and after a period to see if there is any noticeable difference.

What can I do to make myself feel better?

The body and mood changes that happen before a period are called pre-menstrual tension (PMT) or pre-menstrual syndrome (PMS). No one knows for sure why these changes happen, but they're very common. If they bother you, these suggestions may help.

❀ If you put on a few pounds when you've got a period, you're probably retaining extra water. Cut down on salty foods, which help retain water, and don't drink caffeinated drinks such as coffee, tea or fizzy soft drinks.

❀ If you get cross, irritable or panicky for no real reason, or if you suddenly feel weak, particularly in the week before a period, notice whether this happens when you haven't eaten for a long time. If so, eat snacks at short intervals throughout the day, as well as your usual meals, to give you extra energy. Try spending some time on your own to relax. Listen to music, read a book or magazine, watch a film or take a long bath.

❀ If you feel especially tired or lazy, try to get some extra rest and sleep in the fortnight before your period is due. It may also help to eat plenty of vegetables and fruit, wholemeal bread, nuts and seeds.

My moods are more affected by whether I have a good or bad day at school and have a good or bad social life than by my periods.

✿ If you have sweet-food cravings, eat peanuts, peanut butter or ripe bananas, and drink fresh orange juice, herbal teas or lots of water, rather than binge on biscuits or sweets. Doing some light exercise such as a short jog, a dance class or some yoga can make you feel more energetic and will help you to sleep better. Exercise also helps get rid of period pains.

If none of these suggestions helps, it's worth going to see your doctor. Take your menstrual-cycle chart with you. It will help the doctor see how your symptoms relate to your cycle.

Chapter 4

What Are Periods Like?

When will I get my first period?

Most girls start their periods between the ages of nine and fourteen, but you might start earlier or later than that – everyone is different. You can get a good idea of when you might start your period by asking your mum when she started hers, as many girls start their periods at a similar age to their mum. Periods usually start about three years after breast buds have developed, and two to four years after pubic hair starts to grow.

What signs tell me that my period will start soon?

Your breasts may feel slightly more tender a couple of months before you start your periods. Many girls notice a slight white discharge a few months before they start their periods. This is a vaginal discharge and is a normal and healthy sign that the sex hormones are becoming active. This is how one girl describes it:

Six months before I started, I sometimes got a slight white discharge that stained my knickers.

Quite a few girls do have a warning that something is happening just before they get their first period – even if they don't know what it is.

> *I had an ache low down in my tummy and felt tired, and then my period started.*

> *I felt uncomfortable and as if I wanted to pee all the time. I didn't feel ill, but I didn't feel well. Then I discovered my periods had started.*

> *One night I had strange cramps and couldn't sleep. When I got up the next morning, I went to the loo and found blood.*

What will my first period be like?

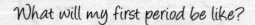

Like any other first experience, you'll probably always remember your first period. Some girls feel excited, because it's something they've been looking forward to.

I had my first period when I was eleven. I was watching TV in my pyjamas. When I got up to go to bed, there was blood on them. My sister, aged ten, said, 'You lucky thing, you've started your periods.' I went upstairs and put on a sanitary towel (which I'd practised doing before). I told everyone who would listen. I felt very proud.

For other girls, it can be a terrible shock, particularly if no one has told them about periods. They think they must have hurt themselves or become ill.

I woke up one morning to find blood on the sheets. It really shocked me as I didn't know where it had come from. I thought I was bleeding to death inside. I didn't know it was a period. No one had told me about them.

Sometimes, even if a girl knows about periods, her first one comes as a surprise, without any warning.

I went to the loo and there it was – blood on my knickers.

I woke up one morning and there was blood on my bed.

No one's first period is exactly the same. When your first period happens, it might be long or short, painful or painless and the flow may be red, rusty or brown. See how these girls' experiences differed.

I bled for two whole weeks. I couldn't believe it.

It was very, very dark brown and very smooth and very thick.

I had bad stomach aches in PE but I didn't notice any blood until I got home. It was a kind of rusty colour.

44

> I was surprised that it didn't hurt and by the way the blood came out bit by bit and didn't pour out as I had expected.

> It wasn't red like real blood. It only lasted a day or two.

What do I need to do when I start?

The most important thing to remember is that periods happen to every single girl and woman and there's no need to panic or feel shy about asking for help. Most women will be kind and do their best to help you. Periods can start at any time and not necessarily when you're best prepared for them. You're most likely to notice you've started when you're in the loo and see bloodstains on your pants. If you're at home, your mum, sister, gran or carer can show you what to do. If you're at school, ask the school nurse, a teacher or a friend for help.

I went to the loo
and there was some blood.
I yelled for my mum
and she came and gave
me a sanitary towel.

I started at the
swimming pool at school.
I had a stomach ache and
could see blood coming out of me.
I told the male teacher
I was going to the toilet. I saw
a female teacher and
told her I'd started.
She gave me a pad.

If you're somewhere where you feel it's impossible to ask for help, you can always make do (see page 83). But if you can talk to someone, you'll avoid having experiences like these.

I was staying with a friend. In the morning, I found blood when I went to the loo. I knew what it was, but I didn't know what to do. I had no sanitary towels or anything and I was too shy to ask or tell anyone. I stuffed loo paper in my pants and hoped that all my layers of clothes would keep the blood hidden.

I got a towel out of a machine in the school toilets. It was folded in a square. I didn't know how to put it on. So I put it in my pants just as it was – in a small square. When I got home, my mum showed me what to do.

What's a normal period?

There's no such thing! The only thing that's certain is that periods start and stop by themselves. Some may last two days; some may last eight days. The flow is usually a slow trickle with an occasional spurt. You can't control it. Unlike peeing, a period happens automatically and continues both day and night.

How much will I bleed?

Sometimes periods are heavy – sometimes they're light. How much blood there is varies from person to person and month to month. If there's a good deal of blood, that's just as healthy as not very much (your body soon replaces whatever blood you lose). Sometimes the flow may be heaviest for the first two days and then taper off, and sometimes it might be exactly the opposite. The amount of blood you lose is actually very little – the equivalent of between four and eight teaspoons. It just looks like more because it's mixed up with mucus and discharge.

Periods are considered heavy if:

❀ you need (rather than choose) to use more than six towels or tampons a day, every day of your period, and/or

❀ your period lasts for much more than a week, and/or

❀ you have more than one period a month and you feel tired and sleepy, even though you're eating well and sleeping normally.

Heavy periods can be caused by shock or worry or upset to your normal routine – such as changing schools, going on holiday and so on. On the other hand, they could mean that your uterus is not working quite the way it should. If your periods suddenly become heavier and you can't think of a good reason, it is a good idea to see a doctor. The doctor might suggest that you eat extra amounts of some iron-rich foods such as brown bread, eggs and watercress, or they might prescribe iron tablets.

What does a period look like?

The colour of the flow may change during your period. It often starts rusty red, becomes bright red when the flow is fastest and then turns brownish by the end. Although the flow may look only like blood, in fact blood makes up only half of it. The rest includes the remains of the extra lining of the uterus and sticky mucus from the cervix and vagina.

I NEVER REALLY THOUGHT ABOUT A CYCLE. BUT I SEE MY PERIODS AS A SIGN THAT MY BODY IS WORKING AS IT SHOULD BE.

How often will I have periods?

For the first two years after your periods start, there will probably be no regular pattern to them. It's quite normal to have a period once every three, four, five or even every six weeks, or to have a period one month and not the next. Hormones send messages to make the lining of your uterus thicken, but the messages are often irregular. After a couple of years, as your hormones settle down, you should begin to notice a more regular pattern to your periods. If your periods are irregular, you might find it helpful to carry a towel or tampon with you so that you're not caught out if you start when you're not expecting to (see Chapter 5 for more information on towels and tampons). It's also helpful to know the signs that your period might start soon – in the few days before your period starts, you might notice a white discharge, slightly tender breasts or mild stomach cramps.

As your ovaries mature, you'll begin ovulating – where a ripe egg bursts out of an ovary (see page 30). You won't necessarily ovulate every month at first, perhaps just every two or three. Once you ovulate regularly every month or so, you should notice a more definite pattern to your cycle, and your periods will probably become heavier. Some people have periods every twenty-one days and some people have them every thirty-five days. Most people have them somewhere in between.

Lots of things can upset your cycle, such as illness or an emotional upset; sudden changes such as travelling, moving school or house; hard physical work, or exams or a crash diet. Your periods might stop completely for a while, or you may have lighter or heavier periods than usual. After a break, you might find that your cycle becomes longer or shorter than it was before.

Should I worry about irregular periods?

For the first couple of years after you start your period, your periods are likely to be very irregular. Once you have a regular cycle, you need to worry about irregular periods only if:

❁ the pattern changes for no good reason and becomes much heavier or lighter.

❁ you miss two periods in a row – and there's no chance of your being pregnant.

❁ you miss one period and think you might be pregnant.

It's worth going to the doctor for a check-up about any of these.

What if I have bleeding between periods (spotting)?

If you notice any bleeding between periods, you should always see a doctor about it, because it's not a usual thing to happen. If it's only light spotting during the middle of the cycle, it's probably to do with ovulation. At this time, some people have a slight pain in either the right or left side of their tummy. This is a sign that the egg is leaving the ovary. However, if the pain lasts for more than a day or so, it might be a sign of illness, so it's worth going to see a doctor.

What if I feel faint during my period?

Occasionally, girls feel faint during their periods. If this happens to you, have some early nights and avoid standing up for long stretches of time – sit down or walk around instead. When you feel faint, sit down with your head between your knees until you feel better, and then have a drink of cold water. Alternatively, lie flat on the floor with your feet resting on a chair, or your bent knees hugged to your chest.

What if my breasts feel sore during a period?

Sore breasts are quite common before and during a period. It doesn't mean anything is wrong with them. Fluid builds up in them as a result of hormone changes and may make them feel more tender. After your period, your breasts will go back to normal.

These changes often go completely unnoticed. If they bother you, wear a slightly bigger bra and have a soak in a warm bath.

On the whole, your breasts won't feel lumpy after a period. If they do, it may be normal, but it would be a good idea to see a doctor.

> *Before a period, my breasts get bigger and my nipples get sore. I have to wear a bigger bra.*

> *Usually for a week before my period my boobs feel very lumpy and tender.*

What if I have a vaginal discharge before a period?

It's quite normal to have a vaginal discharge before a period and also when you ovulate (mid-way between periods). A normal vaginal discharge is a small amount of white or colourless fluid.

When should I see a doctor about vaginal discharge?

❀ If it becomes discoloured (yellow or blood-stained) and smelly. First check you haven't left a tampon in.

❀ If it becomes much thicker and heavier.

❀ If you get a constant sore, burning or itching feeling.

A doctor can quickly tell whether a discharge is normal or not. You may have nothing wrong at all. Or you may have a common infection called thrush, which can be easily treated.

THRUSH

Thrush is a yeast infection which most women get at some point in their lives, and which some women get regularly. Symptoms of thrush include an itchy white discharge and soreness around the vulva. You can buy very effective creams and pills to treat thrush from any pharmacy, but it's worth checking with your doctor first if you have a discharge, to make sure you're getting the right treatment.

What if my periods haven't started yet?

This is amenorrhoea – pronounced a-men-or-eea. If you haven't started your periods yet and most of your friends have, don't worry. It doesn't mean you won't. It just means your body timetable is different from theirs. Sometimes girls don't start until they're sixteen or seventeen, like these girls.

I started developing early, with the exception of my periods. My mum told me all about them when I was ten and gave me some sanitary towels to put away until I needed them — but nothing happened. I had my first bra, but still no periods. I wondered if I was normal. The longer I waited, the more I worried. At first, only a few of my friends started, then almost all of them. Everyone assumed I'd started, so I couldn't confide in anyone. My mum told me not to worry and so did the doctor, but nothing could reassure me. Every time I had something like a tummy ache, I thought my periods were starting, but they never did. I had all sorts of fantasies about what was wrong. The doctor couldn't find anything wrong at all. When I was fifteen, she told me to wait another six months then come back to see her. Finally, three months later, I had my first period — what an anti-climax. I was nearly sixteen.

My periods didn't begin until I was seventeen. As far as my friends were concerned, I'd started three years before, when most of them began theirs. I'd been pretending for three years, because I didn't want them to laugh at me for being a late starter. I couldn't understand why I didn't have periods like them. I noticed that every so often my friends would ask to be excused from swimming and showers after games. Every so often I'd do the same. The times I chose to be excused, I'd also make a point of complaining of tummy ache and all the other things my friends seemed to do. Unfortunately, my PE teacher kept a note of who was excused showers and when. She mentioned to the school doctor that my periods were totally irregular. I was found out. I had to admit that it was all a pretence. I felt better, though, having told someone. It wasn't long after this that my periods actually started. Once I'd started and saw what was involved, I wondered why I'd ever been so anxious to start!

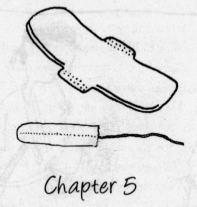

Chapter 5

What Should I Use? Towels and Tampons

Once you start having periods, you'll need to wear something to catch the flow of blood. The flow is usually a slow trickle with an occasional spurt. You can't control it. Unlike peeing, a period happens automatically and continues both day and night. To avoid staining your clothes, you can use either sanitary towels (also known as pads) or tampons. Both sanitary towels and tampons absorb the flow of blood – sanitary towels are worn outside your body, and tampons are worn inside your vagina.

Where do I buy towels and tampons?

All supermarkets and chemists, and many corner shops, sell towels and tampons. If you go to a supermarket or chemist and look in the 'feminine hygiene' section, you'll see a huge range of towels and tampons for sale. If you feel at all embarrassed about buying sanitary products, it might be an idea to ask whoever does the weekly food shop to add some towels or tampons to the shopping list.

How do I know which product to use?

Most manufacturers of towels and tampons have useful websites with information about the different products they make. Some of these websites include a helpful 'product selector', which asks you questions about how heavy your period is, your age and what sort of products you prefer, and then suggests a particular product that might be suitable for you. Some manufacturers occasionally offer free samples through their websites, so you can try out several brands to see which you prefer. It's a good idea to try out a few different products to find out which you like using the best.

Sanitary towels

Sanitary towels are soft, absorbent pads that you put inside your pants. They have a leak-proof plastic backing with a sticky strip so you can press them firmly in place on your pants. Towels come in many different sizes and shapes. Try out different kinds to see which ones suit you the best.

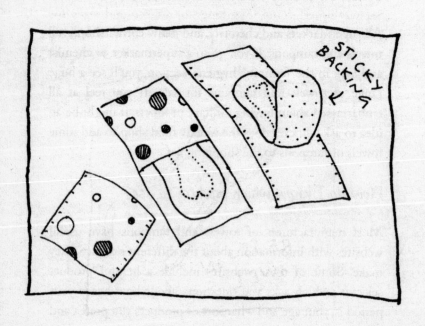

Pantyliners are the thinnest. You might like to use these on the day you expect your period to start or at the end of your period when the flow is very light. You might also like to use them to keep you feeling fresh on days when you have a discharge or as extra protection from leaking when you're using a tampon.

Sanitary towels come in a range of shapes and sizes for light to heavy flow. Towels come in a range of lengths and thicknesses. Different brands use different names

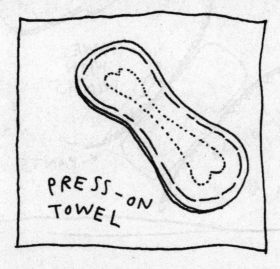

to describe their products, but most manufacturers have products ranging from something like 'ultra-thin' or 'regular' to 'maxi' or 'super'. You will probably find that slim or regular ones give you enough protection. 'Maxi' or 'super' pads are generally for women who have a very heavy flow. Many brands also make extra-long pads which you might find useful for night-time. Most towels have a droplet score on the packet to show how absorbent they are – the more droplets on the packet, the more absorbent the towels are.

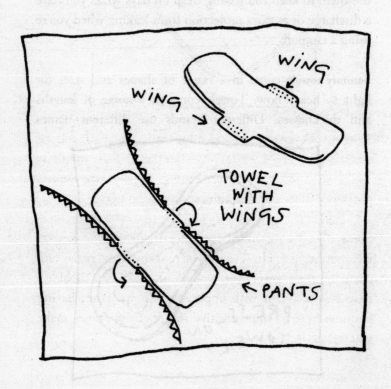

Winged towels have sticky 'wings' which fold under pants to stop the towel moving. Some girls find these very effective, especially for night-time, but others find the wings come unattached and end up feeling bulky and uncomfortable.

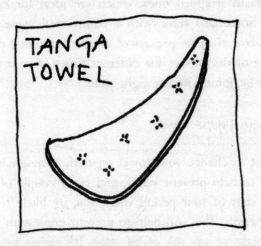

Tanga towels are wider at the front than at the back and are designed to be used with thong-style pants. These might be useful when you want to wear a thong, but will give you less protection than a longer, thicker or winged towel.

Some towels have added fragrance that might make you feel more secure. However, if you're washing every day and changing your towel every couple of hours you shouldn't have any problems with unpleasant odours. Also, having perfume next to your sensitive skin can sometimes make you feel itchy.

Buying towels

You can buy towels in chemists, supermarkets and many corner shops. They come in packets of loose towels or individually-wrapped ones, which are ideal for carrying about. Some also come with a handy fresh wipe. Many manufacturers make packets of towels containing pads in a range of thicknesses for different times of your period, e.g. the beginning, end or night-time.

Changing your towel

It's best to change your towel regularly throughout your period to help prevent stains, and every couple of hours at the start of your period when you are likely to bleed more heavily. This will help to prevent unpleasant smells, sore thighs or any risk of infection. It's easiest to change them in the loo. Remember to wash your hands before and afterwards.

Tampons

A tampon is a tight roll of absorbent cotton and/or rayon fibres with a cord attached to one end. You push it into your vagina and leave it there to soak up the blood-flow inside your body. The muscles of your vagina hold the tampon in place. The tampon expands gently, both in length and width, inside the vagina, but you shouldn't be able to feel that it's there at all.

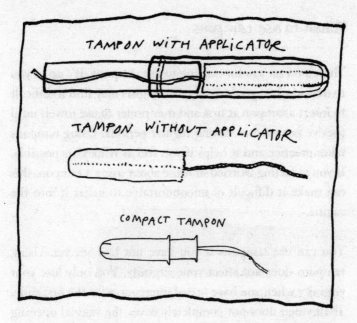

There are two kinds of tampon – those with a cardboard or plastic applicator, which helps you guide the tampon into place, and those without an applicator, which you push in place with your finger. There are also tampons with a 'skirt' for extra protection, as well as scented tampons.

Tampons come in several sizes and absorbencies – small, extra-thin mini-tampons designed specifically for younger girls, lite, regular, super and super-plus. It's important to always use the lowest absorbency tampon for your flow. Begin with the smallest tampons. If they become fully absorbed in less than four hours, you will need to use regular or super ones instead. But if you take out a regular or super tampon after a few hours and there is a lot of white fibre showing, use smaller ones instead.

When to use tampons

There's no set age for starting to use tampons. It's up to you to decide when you're ready. Some girls may find it difficult to insert a tampon at first and may prefer to use towels until they've got used to having regular periods. Using tampons takes practice and it helps if you feel as relaxed as possible. If you're feeling worried or tense about using a tampon, this can make it difficult or uncomfortable to insert it into the vagina.

You can use tampons if you have not had sex yet. Using tampons does not affect your virginity. You only lose your virginity when you have sexual intercourse for the first time. The hymen does not completely cover the vaginal opening and will usually stretch to allow a tampon to go inside the vagina.

I think I pushed the tampons in too gently at first. I became frustrated when they didn't magically slot into place. It took quite a while before I got the hang of it.

I thought that my vagina was very narrow and that anything going in or coming out would hurt — happily I discovered that's not the case.

The anus (the opening where poo comes out) and the urethra (the opening where pee comes out) are separate from the vagina, so using a tampon will not affect pooing and peeing.

Some parents may have cultural or religious beliefs against girls using tampons and this may be a slightly touchy subject. If you want to try using tampons and your parents don't approve, or if you think they might object, talk to your friends instead. See if they use tampons and find out what they think of them.

I bought a packet of tampons to try. I couldn't get the hang of them. I asked my mum for advice. She said I was too young to use them. A few months later, I went to stay with a friend, who suggested that we went swimming. I said I had my period and couldn't. My friend used mini-tampons. She asked her mum if it would be OK if I used them. She said, 'Yes, by all means, they're perfectly harmless.' This surprised me after my mum's reaction. Anyway, I tried them and I've used them ever since.

Discovering your vagina

If you have a problem putting in your first tampon, it might help to get to know your body a bit better first.

If you want to use tampons, it's a good idea to get a feel of what your vagina is like first. Do this when you are relaxed and have a quiet moment on your own, perhaps after a warm bath. Wash your hands before parting the lips of your vulva and putting a finger or two inside your vagina. Feel which direction the vagina goes in. Can you feel that it goes at an angle, more towards your back than straight up? This is the angle to aim at when you put in a tampon. Feel the muscles of the vagina walls. These will hold the tampon securely in place.

The main problem was that I didn't really know where my vagina was, so I didn't know where the tampon went.

Putting in a tampon

When you decide you're ready to try putting in a tampon, make sure you're relaxed and have plenty of time and privacy. If you're tense and in a hurry, your muscles will tighten up! The best time to try is actually during a period, not between periods. You may find it easiest of all during the first two days of a period when the flow is usually heaviest. It's far easier to slide a tampon into a moist vagina than into a dry one. If you find you can't get the tampon in, don't worry. Wait a month or so and then try again until you succeed.

Every packet of tampons contains a leaflet which explains exactly how to put them in. Read it carefully before you try. The instructions may seem complicated at first. Once you get used to putting in a tampon, you will be able to do it in a matter of seconds.

You may like to read the simplified instructions on the following pages, so you can see what's involved.

I was really scared and didn't push them high enough at first. Now they're OK.

It took me six months before my muscles stopped tensing around them. Now I find them easy to use.

How to use a tampon without an applicator

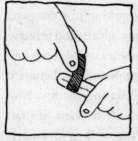

1. Wash your hands. Unwrap the colour tear-strip and the cellophane cover. Gently pull the cord to make sure it is firmly in place. If the cord isn't secure, use another tampon. If you drop the tampon on the floor, don't use it!

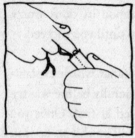

2. Flare out the cord end of the tampon, making a little dimple to put your first finger in.

3. Relax and get into a comfortable position. Sit on the loo with your knees wide apart, stand with your knees bent and legs apart or stand with one foot on the toilet seat.

4. The vagina slopes upwards and backwards, so push the tampon towards the small of your back, as far as it will go into the vagina. Make sure the cord is hanging outside your body.

5. If the tampon is in the right place, you shouldn't be able to feel it at all. If you can feel it, it probably isn't in far enough. Using your index finger gently push the tampon a little further into your vagina or pull it out and try again with a new one. The muscles in your vagina hold the tampon in place, so it can't fall out.

6. To remove a tampon, gently pull on the cord at the same angle as when you put it in. The tampon will slide out and you can throw it away.

How to use a tampon with an applicator

Some tampons have a pair of cardboard or plastic tubes. These are called an applicator. They help you to position the tampon.

1. Wash your hands and unwrap a tampon. Make sure the cord is showing outside the smaller tube.

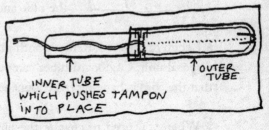

INNER TUBE
WHICH PUSHES TAMPON
INTO PLACE

OUTER TUBE

2. Relax and get into a comfortable position. Sit on the loo with your knees wide apart, stand with your knees bent and legs apart or stand with one foot on the toilet seat.

3. Hold the larger tube (which contains the tampon) at the grooves. With your other hand, spread the lips of your vulva apart. Place the tip of the outer tube of the applicator (not the end with the cord hanging out) on the opening to your vagina.

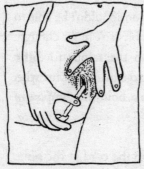

4. Push the outer tube gently into your vagina. The vagina slopes upwards and backwards, so point it towards the small of your back. Don't force it in further than it will go easily. Push it until most of the outer tube is in your vagina.

5. Keep holding the outer tube at the grooves. Put your forefinger over the end of the inner tube to hold the cord in place. Push the inner tube completely into the outer tube, so the ends are level. This pushes the tampon out of the tube and into the vagina.

6. Let go of the cord. Remove both tubes and put them in a disposal unit. Cardboard tubes can be flushed away. Check that the cord is hanging freely outside your body.

7. When you need to change the tampon, gently pull the cord to remove it at the same angle as when you put it in.

8. Applicator tampons also come in compact versions that are more discreet to carry around. They work in the same way as a normal applicator tampon, but you have to slide the inner tube out a little before you insert it.

Changing tampons

··

❀ You need to change a tampon every four to eight hours. In the first few days of your period, when the flow is usually the heaviest, you may want to try using a tampon with a higher absorbency, such as a super or super-plus tampon.

❀ You can tell when a tampon needs changing, because you will notice a kind of bubbling feeling at the base of your vagina or you will see that the cord is blood-stained.

❀ Never leave a tampon in for more than eight hours.

❀ Make absolutely sure that you've removed a used tampon before you put in a new one, and don't forget to take out the last tampon of a period. If you notice an unpleasant odour, even though you've washed thoroughly, check to see whether you've left a tampon in. An odour from your vagina may not be because of a tampon but could be a sign of an infection which needs to be treated. If you haven't left a tampon in and have an odour from your vagina, it's best to get it checked by a doctor.

❀ If you have a heavy flow, you might want to use a towel as well as a tampon, particularly at night. If the tampon cannot absorb any more blood, the towel will catch any blood not absorbed by the tampon.

❁ If you use tampons at night, insert a fresh tampon just before going to bed and remove it as soon as you wake up in the morning. If you sleep for more than eight hours, you should use a pad at night instead of a tampon.

❁ Never insert more than one tampon at a time.

Facts about tampons

Tampons shouldn't be painful to put in. If it hurts when you put one in, it's probably because you haven't aimed it at quite the right angle. The vagina is very stretchy – remember, it can stretch wide enough to let a baby's head come through.

❁ Tampons can't get 'lost' inside you. The opening to the uterus is so tiny that it is impossible for a tampon to go through it. A tampon will always stay in the vagina. There is nowhere else for it to go.

❁ If, by mistake, you push the cord up into your vagina, you can still pull out the tampon. Squat down and put your first two fingers (well washed) into your vagina. If you can't reach the tampon, try pushing hard, as if you were going to the toilet. Then you should be able to grasp it. If you still can't reach it, try again in the bath or ask someone to help you. Doctors and nurses are quite used to taking out tampons.

I FIND IT DIFFICULT TO TELL WHEN
TO CHANGE THEM — SOMETIMES I
FEEL THEM LEAKING AND THEN
IT'S TOO LATE.

Getting rid of used towels and tampons

Towels should always be put in a bag or wrapped up in toilet paper and put in the bin. Some tampons can be flushed down the toilet – it's important to look at the instructions on the packet to find out what you have to do with the kind of tampons you use. Some can be flushed away and others need to be put in the bin. Even if the packet says you can flush them down the loo, it's best to put them in a bin anyway. Flushing towels and tampons down the toilet can block the pipes up and isn't very ecological – imagine how polluting to our oceans these must be.

When you're throwing away towels or tampons, wrap them up tightly in a plastic bag or some loo paper first. Almost all public toilets have special bins called 'sanitary disposal units' for throwing away towels and tampons. There should be bins like these in your school toilets. Some public loos also provide little plastic bags for you to use. When you're at home or at a friend's house, it's best to throw towels and tampons away in the bin. It's helpful to carry a couple of plastic bags with you when you've got your period to put your used tampons or towels in. A normal plastic shopping bag will do, but you can also buy small, scented plastic bags from the same aisle where you find towels and tampons.

AT NIGHT I WEAR A TOWEL. IT'S MORE COMFORTABLE AND GIVES BETTER PROTECTION. IN THE DAY I WEAR TAMPONS.

Towels or tampons – which to use?

Both towels and tampons have advantages and disadvantages. You'll need to try both to discover which you find easier and more comfortable to use. Here's what girls say about them.

Towels

Advantages

❀ They're discreet, secure and I feel confident wearing them.

❀ They are comfortable and easy to use. I don't think I'd like to try tampons yet. They frighten me a little, but I don't know why.

✿ It's easy to know when to change them.

Disadvantages

✿ Sometimes blood leaks over the side and stains my knickers.

✿ I always worry they'll start to smell if I can't change them often enough.

✿ They sometimes slip out of place and rub the top of my thighs.

Tampons

Advantages

✿ Using tampons makes a period easier. They're invisible. There's no worrying about smells or disposal. They make me feel more comfortable and relaxed.

✿ They get rid of that messy feeling.

✿ I like tampons because I can wear them when I go swimming.

Disadvantages

✿ I find it hard to put them in when my flow is light.

✿ Tampons aren't enough for me at night-time. I use a towel as well.

✿ Just occasionally, I find I get the angle wrong when I'm putting one in. It kind of bends over and becomes uncomfortable – in which case I replace it with another.

Be prepared

✿ Make a note in your diary or calendar of the first day of your period, so you know roughly when the next one will happen.

81

✿ Carry a towel or a tampon with you when you're out or at school around the time your period is likely to start. You may even prefer to wear a pantyliner, in case your period starts when you're nowhere near a toilet.

IF YOU DON'T NEED THE PAD OR TAMPON, YOU MAY FIND IT COMES IN HANDY FOR ONE OF YOUR FRIENDS.

❀ Wear dark clothes and knickers during the week or so before your period is likely to start, so that if your period starts when you don't expect it to the blood won't show through.

❀ If your periods are very irregular, or if it would help you feel more prepared, you could always keep a spare towel or tampon in your school bag or in your locker. Even if you don't need the towel or tampon, you may find it comes in handy for one of your friends. A spare pair of pants is useful as well.

❀ If your period starts when you least expect it, use tissues, folded sheets of toilet paper or a clean hanky. Use them like a sanitary towel.

❀ Don't feel embarrassed to ask other girls or women if they have a spare towel or tampon you can use. They all have periods too, so they'll be sympathetic. If you start at school, either the medical room or the office is usually the place to go for supplies. Some schools and public toilets have slot machines where you can buy individual towels or tampons.

TOXIC SHOCK SYNDROME

A rare disease, called toxic shock syndrome (TSS), has been linked with using tampons. Although toxic shock syndrome is uncommon, it can be very serious, can develop very quickly and can sometimes cause death, so it's important to be aware of the symptoms and to know what to do if you think you have any of them.

SYMPTOMS OF TSS
Many of the symptoms of TSS are similar to a bad case of the flu and can include some or all of the following:

✿ a sudden high temperature, of 102°F (39°C) or higher
✿ vomiting
✿ diarrhoea
✿ a rash that looks like sunburn
✿ fainting or feeling faint
✿ muscle aches
✿ dizziness
✿ confusion

WHAT SHOULD I DO IF I HAVE ANY OF THESE SYMPTOMS?
If you get any of these symptoms while you're using a tampon, take it out straight away and see a doctor immediately, even if this means going to an accident and emergency department in a hospital. Tell the doctor that you have been wearing a tampon and that you think you might have TSS.

PREVENTING TSS

Tampon-related TSS is associated with tampon absorbency – the lower the absorbency, the lower the TSS risk; the higher the tampon absorbency, the higher the TSS risk. That's why it's important to use the lowest possible absorbency suitable for your period flow.

WAYS TO HELP AVOID TSS

Always use a tampon with the lowest absorbency suitable for your period flow – if there is a lot of white fibre showing when you remove a tampon, you can probably use a tampon with a lower absorbency.

✿ Use a sanitary towel or pantyliner instead of a tampon from time to time during your period.

✿ Always wash your hands before and after inserting a tampon.

✿ Change your tampon as often as possible during the day. Never wear a tampon for longer than eight hours.

Chapter 6

Looking After Yourself

As you grow up, the hormones that cause your periods to start also affect other parts of your body as well as your moods, your appetite and your energy. You'll need to start looking after yourself in ways you never had to bother about when you were younger.

Keeping clean

You have sweat glands all over your skin. When you get hot, your body perspires to help cool you down. The perspiration is a mixture of water and salt and doesn't smell. At puberty, new sweat glands develop under the arms, around the nipples, navel and in the inner lips of the vulva. These are scent glands, which give you your individual smell, but if you get too hot and sweaty the smell becomes stale.

✿ Have a warm shower or bath daily to keep you feeling clean and fresh. Particularly remember to wash under your arms and between your legs.

✿ Always wash your vulva and bottom from front to back. Then you won't infect your vagina with any of the germs from the anus. Always wipe your bottom from front to back after going to the loo as well.

✿ Change into clean pants after a wash or bath. Cotton ones are best, because synthetic ones tend to keep in heat and moisture unless they have a cotton gusset.

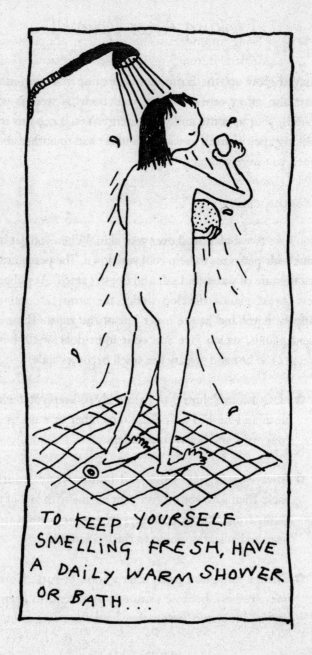

TO KEEP YOURSELF
SMELLING FRESH, HAVE
A DAILY WARM SHOWER
OR BATH...

❁ Start using an underarm deodorant or antiperspirant
   – particularly during a period, when your sweat glands
   are more active. Deodorants and antiperspirants come
   in a spray, stick or roll-on. Deodorants cover up the
   smell of stale sweat. Antiperspirants clog the pores and
   stop you sweating so much in the first place.

Can I have a bath during my period?

You may hear people say you shouldn't wash your hair or
have a bath when you've got a period. Rubbish! It's quite
OK to have a bath, and the flow mostly stops while you're
sitting in the water anyway.

❁ If you use tampons, you can leave one in while you're
   bathing, but put in a clean one afterwards.

❁ If you use sanitary towels, make sure you have one
   handy for when you come out of the bath. Pat your
   vulva dry with tissues or loo paper before you use it.

How often should I change my towel or tampon?

Menstrual blood begins to smell slightly when it reaches the air, and the warmth of your body increases the smell, so it's important to change your towel or tampon regularly.

- ✿ Change your towel three or four times a day, and maybe even more at the beginning of your period when the flow is heaviest.

- ✿ Change your tampon at least every four hours during the day. Never wear a tampon for more than eight hours.

If your pants get blood on them, the best way to get rid of any stains is to soak and rub them in cold, salty water before you wash them.

How can I prevent spots?

The hormones whizzing around your body make your skin glands particularly active. The extra oil they produce can clog the pores and give you spots on your face and sometimes your back as well.

- ✿ Wash your face morning and night with medicated soap and warm water to unclog pores. Then use a toning lotion to tighten up the pores again.

I HAVE REALLY BAD
SKIN AROUND THE
TIME OF MY PERIODS.

❀ If your face is sensitive to soap, buy a medicated face lotion or cream from a chemist.

❀ If you get spots, some people suggest you should avoid fatty and greasy foods such as chocolate, chips and cheese, and eat plenty of fresh fruit instead. Others think that foods have nothing to do with spots. See for yourself if there's a particular food that makes you come out in spots. If so, avoid it!

❀ Don't pick and squeeze spots however tempting this may be – it may only make them worse! If all else fails, put a dab of medicated make-up on the worst ones and try to forget about them.

Why is my hair more greasy now?

At puberty, the oil glands in your scalp that keep your hair healthy often start working overtime and make your hair greasy instead.

- ❀ Choose a shampoo for greasy hair. Give your hair only one wash and make sure you rinse all the shampoo out.

- ❀ Use conditioner only on the ends of your hair.

- ❀ Avoid using lots of products in your hair. Gels and mousses can build up in your hair, weighing it down and making it greasy.

CARE FOR YOUR HAIR

CHOOSE A SHAMPOO FOR GREASY HAIR. GIVE YOUR HAIR ONLY ONE LATHERING AND MAKE SURE YOU RINSE ALL THE SHAMPOO OUT.

Sleeping well

You may find that you need more sleep than you used to. Your own rhythm is what suits you best – don't fight it or compare it with your friends.

People need different amounts of sleep. You might need nine or ten hours a night, while a friend might need only seven or eight hours, or the other way round. If you find you're particularly tired during your periods, have some early nights.

If you have problems getting to sleep, you may not need as much sleep as you think. It's better to stay up or read in bed until you feel sleepy, rather than going to bed and worrying about not being able to get to sleep.

❀ A cup of chamomile tea or warm milk may help calm you down.

❀ If you can't get to sleep because you're worried about a problem, try to share it with someone else.

❀ Fresh air and exercise during the day will always help you sleep better.

Too much sleep can make you feel just as bad as not enough. Don't stay in bed longer than you need to, particularly if you have period pains. It'll only make you feel worse.

Rest is just as important as sleep

· ·

- ✿ Try to find half an hour or more every day to relax, however pressured you may feel.

- ✿ Lie flat on the floor and let your muscles relax one by one or sit in a chair and concentrate on a spot on the wall.

- ✿ Go for a walk and concentrate on breathing, not on thinking.

- ✿ Lie on your bed with your eyes closed and listen to some relaxing music.

I SAVE UP NICE THINGS TO DO FOR DAYS WHEN I FEEL DOWN — A GOOD BOOK, KNITTING, MAKING THINGS, LISTENING TO MY FAVOURITE MUSIC...

Keeping fit

As you get older, you may find that you put on weight more easily. Regular exercise will help your body stay in good shape.

Try to do at least thirty minutes of exercise where you get out of breath at least three times a week. As well as keeping you fit and healthy, exercise can also help period pains. Any organized sport is good exercise, but anything that keeps you moving will help to keep you in shape – cycling, running, dancing, fast walking, even running up and down the stairs.

Whatever exercise you do, try to do it regularly. Don't find an excuse to give up. If you start to find it boring, try doing it with a friend or to music. If you exercise at the same time every day, say when you get up, it will become as much of a habit as brushing your teeth or washing your face.

You can tone some of your muscles even while you're sitting down:

❁ Clench your buttock and thigh muscles.

❁ Press your feet into the floor.

❁ Circle your arms round and around.

❁ Swing your head gently in a circle, first one way and then the other.

What exercises help period pains?

If you get period pains, doing exercises to loosen and relax you can help. The following exercises are designed to strengthen your tummy and pelvic muscles and should relieve cramps.

You might not notice any difference for the first month or so, but if you do the exercises regularly they should start being effective. Even though it might be the last thing you feel like doing when you've got cramps, any exercise will help get rid of period pains.

Exercise also gives you more energy, makes you feel happier and helps you to sleep better.

Touch your toes

Repeat ten times.

- ❀ Stand straight with your feet apart and your arms stretched out at shoulder height.

- ❀ Keeping your arms straight, swing your right hand down to touch your left foot.

- ❀ Come back to your starting position. Repeat, swinging your left hand down to touch your right foot.

Swing your arms

....

Repeat ten times.

- ✿ Stand in the same starting position as for the 'touch your toes' exercise.

- ✿ Twist your body and both arms to the left, without moving your feet. Keep your arms straight and at shoulder height.

- ✿ Return to the starting position.

- ✿ Twist your body and both arms to the right.

Stretch and bend

Repeat ten times.

❀ Stand with your feet apart and your arms stretched straight above your head.

❀ Bend down and touch your toes, keeping your knees straight.

❀ Return to the starting position with your arms still at full stretch.

Forward bends

....

Repeat ten times.

✿ Sit on the floor with your legs and feet together and
your knees straight. Put your hands on your shoulders.

✿ Stretch forward and put your fingers on your toes (if
you can't reach them at first, bend your knees).

✿ Return to the starting position.

Cat stretch

....

Repeat five times.

❀ Kneel with your hands flat on the floor. Breathe in slowly.

❀ As you breathe out, hump your back, pull in your tummy muscles and look down towards your knees.

❀ Now breathe in. As you do so, lift your head upwards and arch your back at the same time. Keep your arms straight the whole time.

Relax

....

❀ Sit on your heels with your arms in front of you and your knees slightly apart.

❀ Gradually stretch forward until your tummy is stretched right over your legs, your forehead is touching the floor and your arms are stretched as far as they will go.

❀ Relax, and breathe deeply.

What if I get cramps and other pains?

Before you start ovulating, it's unlikely, though not impossible, that you'll have painful periods. Once ovulation happens regularly, you might start having cramps and pains during periods, but not necessarily. In any case, people feel pain quite differently – what one person can bear may be unbearable to someone else.

Many people have discomfort rather than pains:

I get a dragging feeling, but it isn't real pain. I also feel constipated and bloated in the first few days of a period.

I can feel my uterus contracting and tension building up. My stomach feels heavy and aches.

Some people, however, have quite severe pains:

Usually on the first day
I have a lot of pain and an
upset tummy. I feel sick,
often badly enough to have
to go to bed for most
of the day.

The pain is usually to do with the period, but not always. You might be constipated as well. If so, try to eat foods with plenty of fibre (such as brown bread, fruit, salads and raw vegetables). Or it may be because you're worried about your periods or something else. Worry can make you tense and knotted up and makes the pain seem worse. It may even be that you get pain because you're expecting it:

I often get bad period
pains, but if I pretend I haven't
got them they go away.

If you do get pains, don't just grit your teeth and bear them. There are plenty of things you can do to relieve them. Below and on the following pages are some people's suggestions. Try them out and see which ones work best for you.

If the pain is more than you can bear, go to your doctor and ask for advice. There are several medical ways of helping period cramps.

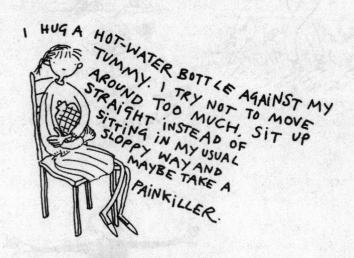

I HUG A HOT-WATER BOTTLE AGAINST MY TUMMY. I TRY NOT TO MOVE AROUND TOO MUCH. SIT UP STRAIGHT INSTEAD OF SITTING IN MY USUAL SLOPPY WAY AND MAYBE TAKE A PAINKILLER.

USUALLY I LIE ON MY BACK WITH MY KNEES UP.

I GO FOR A WALK, DRINK LOTS OF WATER AND HAVE SOME EARLY NIGHTS.

I MAKE SURE I EAT WELL TO KEEP UP MY ENERGY. I ALSO TAKE VITAMIN C.

IF I CAN, I EXERCISE, WHICH ISN'T AT ALL GOOD AT FIRST, BUT IF I SURVIVE, THEN IT'S VERY GOOD!

I MASSAGE MY STOMACH AND BACK. I FIND IT HELPFUL TO PRESS AND RUB THE BOTTOM OF MY SPINE WITH MY KNUCKLES OR FINGERTIPS.

I TRY TO RELAX AND BREATHE DEEPLY.

I TAKE A LONG BATH AND GO TO BED WITH A CUP OF TEA. SOMETIMES LYING ON MY TUMMY HELPS.

And Lastly . . .

We hope that you've found this book useful and will pass it on to anyone else who might find it useful too.

It's important to remember that periods and puberty are a natural part of growing up, and most girls cope very well without too much trouble.

If you're worrying about something, talking to your friends about it is always a good place to start – they might have some helpful advice and you'll often find that they're worrying about exactly the same thing themselves!

If you feel you can't talk to the people around you, try calling one of the helplines listed in the 'useful organizations' section in the following pages. They get lots of calls from young people and are trained to give helpful and confidential advice.

Useful Organizations

Puberty and periods

Brook

www.brook.org.uk

Helpline: 0808 802 1234 (open 9 a.m.–6 p.m., Monday–Friday)

Offers free and confidential advice to young people under twenty-five on sex, periods, puberty and sexual health. Has a free text and online enquiry service. Also provides free sexual-health services.

FPA

www.fpa.org.uk

Helpline (England): 0845 122 8690 (open 9 a.m.–5 p.m., Monday–Friday)

Helpline (Northern Ireland): 0845 122 8687 (open 9 a.m.–5 p.m., Monday–Friday)

Provides information about sex and sexual health, including periods and puberty. Has a free booklet about periods.

Toxic Shock Syndrome Information Service (TSSIS)

www.toxicshock.com

Provides information on TSS, including symptoms and treatment, and information on the link between tampons and TSS.

Sexwise

www.maketherightdecision.co.uk

Helpline: 0800 282 930 (open 7 a.m.–midnight every day)

Free confidential advice line on sex, relationships and contraception for young people aged eighteen or under.

askTheSite
www.thesite.org

Free and confidential online advice service for sixteen to twenty-five-year-olds, run by the useful-information website for young people, www.thesite.org. askTheSite provides answers to questions on a range of subjects, including general health, relationships and sexual health, within three working days.

Health

talkacne
www.talkacne.com

Provides online support and information to people affected by acne.

Terrence Higgins Trust
www.tht.org.uk

Helpline: 0808 802 1221 (open 10 a.m.–10 p.m., Monday–Friday; 12–6 p.m., Saturday and Sunday)

Sexual-health and HIV/AIDS charity providing information, support and advice on HIV/AIDS and sexual health.

Emotional support

....

ChildLine
www.childline.co.uk
Helpline: 0800 1111 (open twenty-four hours)
Free and confidential twenty-four-hour helpline for children
and young people in distress and danger.

Samaritans
www.samaritans.org
Helpline: 0845 790 9090 (open twenty-four hours)
Free and confidential twenty-four-hour helpline providing
emotional support to people who are experiencing feelings
of distress or despair.

No Panic
www.nopanic.org.uk
Helpline: 0800 138 8889 (open 10 a.m.–10 p.m. every day)
Provides support for panic attacks, anxiety and phobias.

Diet and nutrition

....

Eating Disorders Association (Beat)
www.b-eat.co.uk
Helpline: 0845 634 7650 (open 4.30–8.30 p.m. Monday–Friday;
1.30–4.30 p.m. Saturday)
Provides information about eating disorders, where to get help
and how to help someone you know with an eating disorder.

Vegetarian Society

www.vegsoc.org

Provides booklets and information for people wishing to be vegetarian.

Viva

www.viva.org.uk

Campaigns for vegetarianism.

Index

JUDY BLUME

ARE YOU THERE, GOD? IT'S ME, MARGARET

Are you there, God? It's me, Margaret, again. Have you thought about it? My growing, I mean. I've got a bra now. It would be really nice if I had something to put in it.

There are lots of things about growing up that are hard to be honest about, even with your best friends. So Margaret talks to God about her feelings – in one of Judy Blume's funniest and best-known novels.

DEENIE

I hate it when my mother brags about me
and my sister. 'Deenie's the beauty and
Helen's the brain.'

Deenie's not sure that she wants to be a model,
even though her mother is determined to make
her one. Then the doctors tell her she'll have to
wear an ugly brace for four years to straighten her
spine – just when Buddy Brader was beginning
to like her. Deenie is going to need real courage
to face the future . . .